Baked *& Delicious*

First printed 2012
Eaglemoss Publications Group, 1st Floor, Beaumont House,
Kensington Village, Avonmore Road,
London W14 8TS

While every care has been taken in compiling the information in
this book, the publishers cannot accept responsibility for any errors,
inadvertent or not, that may be found or may occur at some time in
the future owing to changes in legislation or for any other reason.

ISSN 978-0-9560894-6-5
123456789

Reproduction by F E Burmans, UK.
Printed in the EU by Imprimerie Pollina.

Baked & Delicious
Cupcakes & Fairy Cakes
Front cover: EM/Tim Hill, 8 EM/Tim Hill (t), EM/Tim Hill (b), 10 EM/
Tim Hill, 16 Bilic/PhotoCuisine, 18 Marielle/PhotoCuisine, 26 Abd/
PhotoCuisine, 32 Gelberger/PhotoCuisine, 42 Viel/PhotoCuisine,
54 Abd/PhotoCuisine (b), Hall/PhotoCuisine (t), 56 Foodfolio/
PhotoCuisine, 60 Fondacci/Markezana, 64 Foodfolio/PhotoCuisine,
71 Bilic/PhotoCuisine, 72 Bagros/PhotoCuisine, 73 Foodfolio/
PhotoCuisine, 74 Rivière/PhotoCuisine, 76 Studio/PhotoCuisine,
78 Photolibrary.com/Fresh Food Images/Tim Hill, 82 Sirois/
PhotoCuisine, 84 Abd/PhotoCuisine, 86 EM/Steve Lee,
92 Foodfolio/PhotoCuisine.

EM = Eaglemoss Publications Group

For more details, go to
www.baked-and-delicious.com

Baked *& Delicious*

Cupcakes &
Fairy Cakes

Cupcakes & Fairy Cakes

Cupcakes have become so popular over recent years – they are served at even the most fashionable weddings and parties. With this book, you too can create these wonderful generously-iced delights as well as smaller, daintier fairy cakes – ideal for birthdays, afternoon tea, celebrations or just an anytime treat.

We've got a great selection of recipes in all kinds of flavours, from classics like vanilla, chocolate and lemon, to more exotic ideas, such as lime, lychee, rose, banana and coconut. Plus, you can choose from lots of different icings – do you prefer rich buttercream, melt-in-the-mouth American frosting, indulgent mascarpone, whipped cream or simple child-friendly glacé icing? The possibilites are endless, so grab a mixing bowl and spoon and get cooking. Happy baking!

The Baked & Delicious Team

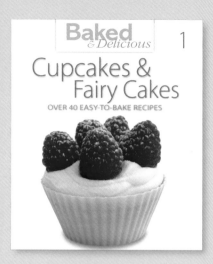

Baked *& Delicious*

1

Cupcakes & Fairy Cakes

OVER 40 EASY-TO-BAKE RECIPES

In this book...

Over 40 delicious cupcake and fairy cake recipes to bake and enjoy – from simple teatime treats to glamorous creations for special occasions. With beautiful photographs, easy-to-follow instructions and useful tips, you are sure of success every time.

Baked *& Delicious*

Contents

Recipes

Frosted Dreams

There are all kinds of delicious toppings you can use on your cupcakes, from simple whipped cream to fancy American frosting. Here are a few tempting ideas to try.

The most popular choice for icing cupcakes is buttercream (see below). This is easy to make, tastes great and you can vary the flavour to match the cupcakes. If you fancy something more complicated, try American frosting (see right) which is crisp on the outside and soft and gooey inside.

FLAVOUR VARIATIONS

You can alter the basic buttercream below with many different flavours. For chocolate cupcakes, omit the vanilla and add a heaped tablespoon of cocoa powder with the sugar.

You can also replace the vanilla with lemon, orange or lime zest, rosewater, almond or mint essence, melted chocolate or fruit purée.

EXTRA RICHNESS

Cream cheese icing is another popular topping and goes really well with rich cupcakes like dark chocolate or red velvet. Beat together 40g (1½oz) softened butter and 125g (4oz) cream cheese until soft. Add 250g (9oz) sifted icing sugar and beat for about 2 minutes until smooth. Don't overbeat as it will become too soft to pipe.

Icing Cupcakes

Makes enough to ice 12 cupcakes
75g (3oz) butter, softened
2 tbsp milk
1 tsp vanilla extract
225g (8oz) icing sugar, sifted
Food colouring, optional

For perfect results, make sure the icing sugar is sifted to avoid lumps and whisk well until smooth. This icing can be piped instead of spread.

1 Beat together the butter, milk, vanilla and half the sugar to combine. Add the remaining sugar and beat until fluffy.

2 Add food colouring if using. Spread a dollop of icing on a palette knife from the top to one side of the cake.

American Frosting

Makes enough to ice up to 24 cakes
2 egg whites
500g (18oz) caster sugar
Pinch of cream of tartar

1 Whisk the egg whites until stiff and dry. Heat the sugar with 4 tablespoons hot water, stirring, until dissolved.

2 Bring to the boil, but don't stir. Cook for at least 10 minutes until thick and syrupy. To test, drop small spoonfuls into cold water – if it is ready, you will be able to shape it into a soft ball. Remove from the heat straight away.

3 Add the cream of tartar and whisk until cloudy. Pour into the egg whites, whisking. Set the bowl over a pan of simmering water and whisk until the frosting is thick and loses its shine.

Decoration Ideas

There are all sorts of sugar sprinkles and shapes available in supermarkets and cake decorating shops to enhance your cakes.

Fruit and berries Fresh fruits, such as summer berries, sliced mango, peach, pineapple, banana (tossed in lemon juice first) or star fruit, make a refreshing change as a topping. Or try crystallised or marzipan fruits instead.

Mascarpone frosting For a quick and easy topping, beat creamy mascarpone to a soft, spreadable consistency, adding a little pineapple juice or syrup from a jar of stem ginger to loosen. Spread over the cake and top with toasted fresh coconut shavings.

3 Repeat step 2 for the other side until the cake is covered with a generous layer of the icing.

4 Working from the centre, move the palette knife anti-clockwise to create a decorative swirl.

Vanilla cupcakes

Prep time: 25 mins + cooling
Cook time: 20 mins
Makes 12 cakes

For the cakes:
125g (4oz) unsalted butter, softened
125g (4oz) caster sugar
2 large eggs, beaten
125g (4oz) self-raising flour, sifted
2 tbsp milk
1 tsp vanilla extract

For the topping:
75g (3oz) unsalted butter, softened
2 tbsp milk
1 tsp vanilla extract
225g (8oz) icing sugar, sifted
Raspberries, to decorate

These light vanilla sponge cakes just melt in the mouth, while the rich buttercream topping and fresh raspberry decoration add an elegant finish.

1 Preheat the oven to 190°C/375°F/gas 5. Stand 12 silicone cases or paper cupcake cases in a 12-hole muffin tin. Beat together the butter and sugar in a large bowl until pale and fluffy.

2 Gradually whisk in the beaten eggs, adding a spoonful of the flour with each addition, to prevent the mixture curdling.

3 Gently fold in the remaining flour with a large metal spoon. Stir in the milk and vanilla extract.

4 Divide the mixture equally between the cases. Bake for 15–20 minutes until well risen and golden. Leave to cool completely on a wire rack.

5 For the topping, beat together the butter, milk, vanilla and half the icing sugar until well combined. Beat in the remaining sugar until the mixture is pale and fluffy. Spread onto the cupcakes (see pages 8/9) and decorate with raspberries.

Rose cupcakes

Prep time: 30 mins + cooling
Cook time: 20 mins
Makes 12 cakes

For the cakes:
125g (4oz) butter, softened
125g (4oz) caster sugar
2 eggs
150g (5oz) plain flour
2 tsp baking powder
3 tbsp milk
½ tbsp rosewater

For the topping:
75g (3oz) butter, softened
200g (7oz) icing sugar
½ tbsp rosewater
Red or pink food colouring
Multicoloured sugar balls

The addition of rosewater gives these pretty cakes a wonderful aroma and delicate flavour. Find it in the baking or world food section of the supermarket.

1 Preheat the oven to 180°C/350°F/gas 4. Stand 12 silicone cases or paper cupcake cases in a 12-hole muffin tin. Beat together the butter and caster sugar in a bowl with an electric whisk or wooden spoon until pale and creamy.

2 Beat in the eggs, one at a time, adding a tablespoon of flour with each one, until well combined. Sift in the rest of the flour and the baking powder. Mix together gently. Beat in the milk and rosewater.

3 Divide the mixture between the cases, filling them about two-thirds full. Bake for 20 minutes until golden and springy to the touch. Leave to cool completely on a wire rack.

4 For the topping, beat together the butter, icing sugar and rosewater until smooth and creamy. Beat in a few drops of colouring to make a pale pink icing.

5 Spoon into a piping bag fitted with a star-shaped nozzle and pipe swirls on top of the cakes. (Alternatively, spread onto the cakes – see pages 8/9.) Sprinkle with sugar balls.

Zingy lemon cupcakes

Prep time: 30 mins + cooling
Cook time: 20 mins
Makes 12 cakes

For the cakes:
125g (4oz) butter, softened
125g (4oz) caster sugar
2 eggs
150g (5oz) self-raising flour

For the topping:
1 unwaxed lemon
100g (3½oz) butter, softened
150g (5oz) icing sugar

These dainty cakes are flavoured with plenty of lemon for extra zing. Using a pale unsalted French butter will give your icing a much lighter colour than standard butter.

1 Preheat the oven to 180°C/350°F/gas 4. Stand 12 silicone cases or paper cake cases in a 12-hole muffin tin. Place the butter and caster sugar In a bowl and beat with an electric whisk until pale and fluffy. Add the eggs, one at a time, beating well each time. Add the flour and gently mix together.

2 Divide the mixture between the cases, filling them about two-thirds full. Bake for 20 minutes until golden and springy to the touch. Leave to cool completely on a wire rack.

3 For the topping, finely grate the zest of the lemon and set aside. Squeeze the juice. Beat together the butter, icing sugar and enough lemon juice to make a soft fluffy icing.

4 Spoon into a piping bag fitted with a large plain nozzle and pipe in swirls on top of the cakes. Sprinkle with the lemon zest.

Blueberry cupcakes

Prep time: 30 mins + cooling
Cook time: 20 mins
Makes 12 cakes

For the cakes:
125g (4oz) self-raising flour, sifted
125g (4oz) caster sugar
125g (4oz) margarine, softened
2 large eggs
½ tsp vanilla extract

For the topping:
250g (9oz) unsalted butter, softened
200g (7oz) icing sugar
Blue food colouring
100g (3½oz) blueberries
2 tbsp double cream, for drizzling

These simple cakes are perfect for a summer party. For an extra boost of flavour, add a sprinkling of dried blueberries to the cake batter and stir in.

1 Preheat the oven to 180°C/350°F/gas 4. Stand 12 silicone cases or paper cupcake cases in a 12-hole muffin tin. Place the flour, caster sugar, margarine, eggs and vanilla in a large bowl and beat with an electric whisk until smooth and creamy.

2 Spoon the mixture into the cases, filling them two-thirds full. Bake for 15-20 minutes until golden and risen. Leave to cool completely on a wire rack.

3 For the icing, beat together the butter and icing sugar until smooth and creamy. Gradually add drops of food colouring, beating well, until you have a violet-coloured icing.

4 Spread the icing on top of the cupcakes (see pages 8/9). Decorate each cake with a few blueberries and a drizzle of double cream around the edge.

Chocolate & pepper cupcakes

Prep time: 35 mins + cooling
Cook time: 20 mins
Makes 12 cakes

For the cakes:
125g (4oz) self-raising flour
25g (1oz) cocoa powder
125g (4oz) butter, softened
125g (4oz) golden caster sugar
2 large eggs
pinch of ground black pepper
pinch of cayenne pepper

For the topping:
100g (3½oz) unsalted butter, softened
100g (3½oz) icing sugar
Dark and milk chocolate balls, to decorate
Chocolate sprinkles, to decorate

These tempting chocolate cupcakes hide a secret inside – a touch of spice from some cayenne and black pepper. You'll be surprised, it really works!

1 Preheat the oven to 180°C/350°F/gas 4. Stand 12 silicone cases or paper cupcake cases in a 12-hole muffin tin. Place the flour, cocoa, butter, caster sugar, eggs, black and cayenne pepper in a large bowl. Beat with an electric whisk until smooth and creamy.

2 Spoon the mixture into the cases, filling each one about two-thirds full. Bake for 15–20 minutes until risen and springy to the touch. Leave to cool completely on a wire rack.

3 For the topping, beat together the butter and icing sugar until smooth and creamy. Spoon into a piping bag fitted with a very small plain nozzle. Pipe onto the cakes in a squiggly shape. Sprinkle with chocolate balls and sprinkles before serving.

Redcurrant cupcakes

Prep time: 40 mins + cooling
Cook time: 30 mins
Makes 12 cakes

For the cakes:
125g (4oz) butter, softened
125g (4oz) caster sugar
2 eggs
150g (5oz) self-raising flour
1 tsp baking powder
4 tbsp milk
1 tsp vanilla extract
125g (4oz) redcurrants, plus extra, to
    decorate

For the caramel drops:
125g (4oz) caster sugar
Squeeze of lemon juice

For the topping:
100g (3½oz) butter, softened
150g (5oz) icing sugar
Pink food colouring

A hidden layer of redcurrants gives these cakes a lovely fruity surprise inside while the sweet caramel drops make a pretty, and tasty, decoration.

1 Preheat the oven to 180°C/350°F/gas 4. Stand 12 silicone cases or paper cake cases in a 12-hole muffin tin. Beat together the butter and caster sugar with an electric whisk until pale and fluffy. Add the eggs, one at a time, adding a spoonful of the flour each time. Beat until well combined. Stir in the flour and baking powder, then mix in the milk and vanilla extract.

2 Place a spoonful of the mixture in each case then scatter over the recurrants. Cover with the rest of the cake mixture. Bake for 20 minutes until golden and springy to the touch. Leave to cool completely on a wire rack.

3 Meanwhile, make the caramel drops. Place the sugar in a pan with 2 tablespoons water and the lemon juice. Heat until the sugar dissolves, then bring to a simmer and cook until it turns a beautiful amber colour. Using a teaspoon, drop tiny blobs of the caramel onto a sheet of greaseproof paper. Leave to cool.

4 For the topping, beat together the butter and icing sugar until smooth, light and creamy. Add food colouring to create a pale pink icing. Spoon into a piping bag fitted with a star-shaped nozzle. Pipe onto the cakes in swirls.

5 Sprinkle immediately with the caramel drops and decorate each cake with a sprig of redcurrants. Chill for 1 hour before serving.

Caramel cupcakes

Prep time: 30 mins + cooling
Cook time: 30 mins
Makes 12 cakes

For the cakes:
125g (4oz) butter, softened
125g (4oz) soft light brown sugar
2 eggs
150g (5oz) self-raising flour
4 tbsp milk
12 small soft caramel sweets

For the caramel sauce:
100g (3½oz) icing sugar
100ml (3½fl oz) double cream

For the topping:
100g (3½oz) butter, softened
150g (5oz) icing sugar
12 sultanas, to decorate

Brown sugar and a creamy caramel sauce give these golden cakes a rich sweet flavour. To save time, you can use a bought caramel sauce, such as dulce de leche.

1 For the caramel sauce, place the sugar in a pan with 2 tablespoons water and heat until dissolved. Bring to a simmer, then cook over a medium heat until it turns an amber caramel colour. Remove from the heat and stir in the cream. Cook gently for 2 minutes. Leave to cool.

2 Preheat the oven to 180°C/350°F/gas 4. Stand 12 silicone cases or paper cake cases in a 12-hole muffin tin. Beat together the butter and brown sugar until pale and fluffy. Beat in the eggs, one at a time. Add the flour and milk and mix until combined.

3 Place a spoonful of the cake mixture in each case, then add a caramel sweet to each one. Top with the remaining cake mixture. Bake for 15–20 minutes until risen and springy to the touch. Leave to cool completely on a wire rack.

4 For the topping, beat together the butter, icing sugar and half the caramel sauce until smooth and creamy. Spoon onto the cakes and swirl with a palette knife. Drizzle on the remaining caramel sauce and decorate with sultanas.

Blue-iced cupcakes

Prep time: 30 mins + cooling
cook time: 20 mins
Makes 12 cakes

For the cakes:
125g (4oz) butter, softened
125g (4oz) caster sugar
2 eggs
150g (5oz) self-raising flour
3 tbsp milk
1 tsp vanilla extract

For the topping:
100g (3½oz) butter, softened
200g (7oz) icing sugar
Blue and pink food colouring
Multicoloured sugar balls

The addition of the orange juice makes these cakes particularly moist and luscious. They are topped with a rich, butter icing and tiny iced sugar balls.

1 Preheat the oven to 180°C/350°F/gas 4. Stand 12 silicone cases or paper cake cases in a 12-hole muffin tin. Beat together the butter and caster sugar with an electric whisk until pale and fluffy. Beat in the eggs, one at a time, adding a spoonful of the flour each time. Stir in the flour, milk and vanilla extract.

2 Divide the mixture between the cases, filling them about two-thirds full. Bake for 20 minutes until golden and springy to the touch. Leave to cool completely on a wire rack.

3 For the topping, beat together the butter, icing sugar and a few drops of blue food colouring until smooth and creamy. Carefully swirl in a little pink colouring with a cocktail stick. Spoon into a piping bag fitted with a star-shaped nozzle and pipe onto the cakes. Sprinkle with sugar balls to decorate.

Pistachio & cherry cupcakes

Prep time: 35 mins + cooling
Cook time: 20 mins
Makes 12 cakes

For the cakes:
125g (4oz) self-raising flour, sifted
125g (4oz) margarine, softened
125g (4oz) caster sugar
2 large eggs
½ tsp vanilla extract
1 tbsp Kirsch (optional)

For the topping:
100g (3½oz) cream cheese
100g (3½oz) icing sugar
200ml (7fl oz) double cream
50g (2oz) white chocolate curls
40g (1½oz) pistachios, crushed
12 cocktail cherries, drained

These luxury cakes are topped with a rich cream cheese frosting. You can add a splash of Kirsch or cherry brandy to the frosting for an extra indulgent kick.

1 Preheat the oven to 180°C/350°F/gas 4. Stand 12 silicone cases or paper cupcake cases in a 12-hole muffin tin. Place the flour, margarine, caster sugar, eggs, vanilla and Kirsch, if using, in a large bowl. Beat with an electric whisk until smooth and creamy.

2 Divide the mixture evenly between the cases, filling about two-thirds full. Bake for 15-20 minutes until golden and risen. Leave to cool completely on a wire rack.

3 For the topping, beat together the cream cheese and icing sugar until smooth. Whip the cream in a separate bowl to soft peaks, then fold into the cheese mixture.

4 Transfer the icing to a piping bag fitted with a star-shaped nozzle and pipe in generous swirls on top of the cupcakes. Sprinkle the white chocolate curls and crushed pistachios on top. Decorate each one with a cocktail cherry before serving.

Red velvet cupcakes

Prep time: 30 mins + cooling
Cook time: 20 mins
Makes 12 cakes

For the cakes:
125g (4oz) butter, softened
125g (4oz) caster sugar
2 eggs
150g (5oz) self-raising flour
1 tsp vanilla extract
4 tbsp milk
10 drops of red food colouring
100g (3½oz) strawberry or raspberry jam

For the topping:
250ml (9fl oz) double cream
2 tbsp icing sugar
12 red sweets or glacé cherries

The fabulous red sponge contrasts beautifully with the white cream topping in these fashionable cupcakes. They work well with cream cheese frosting too (see page 8).

1 Preheat the oven to 180°C/350°F/gas 4. Stand 12 silicone cases or paper cake cases in a 12-hole muffin tin. Beat together the butter and caster sugar until pale and fluffy. Beat in the eggs, one at a time. Stir in the flour, followed by the vanilla, milk, food colouring and jam to make a creamy red mixture

2 Divide the mixture between the cases, filling them about two-thirds full. Bake for 15–20 minutes until risen and springy to the touch. Leave to cool completely on a wire rack.

3 For the topping, whip the cream with the icing sugar until stiff. Spoon into a piping bag fitted with a star-shaped nozzle. Pipe in swirls on the cakes and decorate with sweets or cherries.

Banana-caramel cupcakes

Prep time: 25 mins + cooling
Cook time: 30 mins
Makes 12 cakes

For the cakes:
125g (4oz) butter, softened
125g (4oz) caster sugar
1 banana, peeled
2 eggs
125g (4oz) self-raising flour
½ tsp Chinese 5-spice powder
4 tbsp milk

For the topping:
100g (3½oz) caster sugar
2 bananas, peeled
Juice of ½ lemon
125g (4oz) crème fraîche

Mashed banana and a touch of aromatic spice make these cakes extra tasty. They make a great breakfast treat topped with natural yogurt, bananas and honey.

1 Preheat the oven to 180°C/350°F/gas 4. Stand 12 silicone cases or paper cake cases in a 12-hole muffin tin. Beat together the butter and caster sugar with an electric whisk until pale and fluffy. Mash the banana with a fork and whisk in. Beat in the eggs, one at a time. Stir in the flour and 5-spice. Add the milk.

2 Divide the mixture between the cases, filling them about two-thirds full. Bake for 15–20 minutes until golden and springy to the touch. Leave to cool completely on a wire rack.

3 For the topping, place the sugar in a saucepan with a little water. Heat until the sugar dissolves, then bring to a simmer and cook until it turns an amber caramel colour. Remove from the heat and add 3 tablespoons boiling water. Return to the heat and simmer for 2 minutes. Allow to cool slightly.

4 Slice the bananas and toss with the lemon juice. Place a spoonful of crème fraîche on each cake, then top with banana slices and drizzle over the caramel. Serve immediately.

Fragrant cupcakes with rose

Prep time: 40 mins + cooling
Cook time: 20 mins
Makes 12 cakes

For the cakes:
150g (5oz) self-raising flour
150g (5oz) golden caster sugar
160g (5½oz) margarine, softened
3 large eggs
1 tsp rose extract

For the topping:
150g (5oz) icing sugar
200g (7oz) unsalted butter, softened
1 tsp rose extract
Red or pink food colouring
Red sugar flowers, to decorate

Rose extract adds an exotic fragrance to these pretty cakes. For a special occasion, decorate with fresh or crystallised rose petals instead of sugar flowers.

1 Preheat the oven to 180°C/350°F/gas 4. Stand 12 silicone cases or paper cupcake cases in a 12-hole muffin tin. Place the flour, caster sugar, margarine, eggs and rose extract in a large bowl. Beat together with an electric whisk until smooth and creamy.

2 Divide the mixture evenly between the cases. Bake for 15-20 minutes until golden and springy to the touch. Leave to cool completely on a wire rack.

3 For the topping, beat together the icing sugar, butter and rose extract until smooth. Add a drop of colouring and beat until pale pink in colour.

4 Spoon the icing into a piping bag fitted with a small star-shaped nozzle. Pipe swirls on top of the cupcakes and decorate with red sugar flowers before serving.

Raspberry vanilla cupcakes

Prep time: 30 mins + cooling
Cook time: 20 mins
Makes 12 cakes

For the cakes:
150g (5oz) butter, softened
125g (4oz) caster sugar
2 eggs
125g (4oz) self-raising flour
3 tbsp milk
1 tsp vanilla extract
175g (6oz) raspberries

For the topping:
100g (3½oz) butter, softened
175g (6oz) icing sugar, plus extra, to dust
2 tsp vanilla sugar
White sugar balls, to decorate

A juicy fresh raspberry layer gives these pretty cakes a real boost of flavour. You can add a splash of raspberry liqueur to the icing for extra luxury.

1 Preheat the oven to 180°C/350°F/gas 4. Stand 12 silicone cases or paper cake cases in a 12-hole muffin tin. Beat together the butter and caster sugar until pale and fluffy. Beat in the eggs, one at a time, adding a spoonful of the flour each time. Mix in the remaining flour, milk and vanilla extract.

2 Add a spoonful of mixture to each case then place 3 raspberries in each one. Cover with the rest of the cake mixture. Bake for 15–20 minutes until golden and springy to the touch. Leave to cool completely on a wire rack.

3 For the topping, beat together the butter, icing sugar and vanilla sugar until pale and creamy. Spoon into a piping bag fitted with a star-shaped nozzle and pipe in swirls on the cakes.

4 Decorate each cake with a raspberry then sprinkle with sugar balls and dust with icing sugar before serving.

Almond cupcakes with lemon

Prep time: 30 mins + cooling
Cook time: 25 mins
Makes 12 cakes

For the cakes:
125g (4oz) butter, softened
150g (5oz) caster sugar
Zest of 1 lemon
1 tsp vanilla extract
2 large eggs
150g pot plain natural yogurt
150g (5oz) self-raising flour
50g (2oz) ground almonds

For the topping:
60g (2½oz) butter, softened
200g (7oz) icing sugar
1 tbsp lemon juice
Sugar flowers or crystallised violets, to
    decorate

The addition of ground almonds gives these pretty cakes a lovely moist texture and mild nutty flavour. The tangy lemon icing tastes great and cuts through the richness.

1 Preheat the oven to 180°C/350°F/gas 4. Stand 12 silicone cases or paper cake cases in a 12-hole muffin tin. Beat together the butter, caster sugar, lemon zest and vanilla with an electric whisk until pale and fluffy. Beat in the eggs, one at a time, then stir in the yogurt. Gently stir in the flour and almonds.

2 Divide the mixture between the cases, filling them about three-quarters full. Bake for 20–25 minutes until golden and springy to the touch. Leave to cool completely on a wire rack.

3 For the topping, beat together the butter, icing sugar and lemon juice until smooth and creamy. Spoon onto the cakes and swirl with a palette knife. Decorate with flowers or violets.

Home-style lemon cupcakes

Prep time: 25 mins + cooling
Cook time: 20 mins
Makes 12 cakes

For the cakes:
125g (4oz) butter, softened
125g (4oz) caster sugar, plus extra, to sprinkle
Zest and juice of 1 large unwaxed lemon
2 eggs
150g (5oz) self-raising flour
3 tbsp milk

For the topping:
150g (5oz) icing sugar
1 tsp lemon juice

These lovely lemon cakes are real family favourites – perfect to enjoy anytime. Lemon bonbons make a cute and delicious decoration instead of the zest.

1 Preheat the oven to 180°C/350°F/gas 4. Stand 12 silicone cases or paper cake cases in a 12-hole muffin tin. Beat together the butter and caster sugar until pale and fluffy. Stir in the lemon juice and half the zest. Beat in the eggs, one at a time. Gently mix in the flour and milk.

2 Divide the mixture between the cases, filling them about two-thirds full. Bake for 15–20 minutes until golden and springy to the touch. Leave to cool completely on a wire rack.

3 For the topping, mix together the icing sugar and lemon juice until smooth. (Be patient, this will take a little while but it will mix.) Spoon onto the cupcakes and decorate with the remaining lemon zest and a sprinkling of caster sugar. Allow to set before serving.

Chocolate-orange mini cupcakes

Prep time: 30 mins + cooling
Cook time: 18 mins
Makes 20 cakes

For the cakes:
125g (4oz) butter, softened
125g (4oz) caster sugar
75g (3oz) dark chocolate, melted
2 eggs
150g (5oz) self-raising flour
2 tbsp freshly squeezed orange juice

For the topping:
100g (3½oz) butter, softened
150g (5oz) icing sugar
1–2 teaspoons fresh orange juice
Multicoloured sugar balls, to decorate

These bite-sized cakes are perfect for a childrens' party — although the adults won't be able to resist them either! Add orange colouring to the icing for extra wow factor.

1 Preheat the oven to 180°C/350°F/gas 4. Stand 20 mini silicone cases or paper cake cases in 2 x 12-hole mini muffin tins. Beat together the butter and caster sugar until pale and fluffy. Beat in the melted chocolate then the eggs, one at a time. Stir in the flour and orange juice until well combined.

2 Divide the mixture between the cases, filling them about two-thirds full. Bake for 15–18 minutes until risen and springy to the touch. Leave to cool completely on a wire rack.

3 For the topping, beat together the butter, icing sugar and enough orange juice to make a smooth creamy icing. Spoon into a piping bag fitted with a small star-shaped nozzle. Pipe onto the cakes then decorate with coloured sugar balls.

Chocolate cupcakes

Prep time: 30 mins + cooling
Cook time: 25 mins
Makes 12 cakes

For the cakes:
125g (4oz) self-raising flour
25g (1oz) cocoa powder
125g (4oz) butter, softened
125g (4oz) golden caster sugar
2 large eggs

For the topping:
50g (2oz) milk chocolate, roughly
   chopped
250g (9oz) unsalted butter, softened
150g (5oz) icing sugar
25g (1oz) dark chocolate, grated

No-one will be able to resist these classic chocolate cakes. Melted chocolate gives the icing a wonderful flavour — try using plain or white chocolate for a change.

1 Preheat the oven to 180°C/350°F/gas 4. Stand 12 silicone cases or paper cupcake cases in a 12-hole muffin tin. Place the flour, cocoa, butter, sugar and eggs in a large bowl. Beat together with an electric whisk until smooth and creamy.

2 Divide the mixture evenly between the cases. Bake for 15-20 minutes until risen and springy to the touch. Leave to cool completely on a wire rack.

3 For the topping, place the milk chocolate in a heatproof bowl. Set over a pan of gently simmering water and leave to melt. Cool slightly. Beat together the icing sugar and butter until smooth. Add the melted chocolate and beat until evenly mixed.

4 Spoon the icing into a piping bag fitted with a star-shaped nozzle. Pipe in swirls on top of the cakes. Decorate with the grated dark chocolate before serving.

Luscious lime cupcakes

Prep time: 25 mins + cooling
Cook time: 20 mins
Makes 12 cakes

For the cakes:
125g (4oz) butter, softened
125g (4oz) caster sugar
2 eggs
150g (5oz) self-raising flour
Zest and juice of 1 unwaxed lime

For the topping:
75g (3oz) butter, softened
200g (7oz) icing sugar
Zest of 1 lime, plus 2 tsp juice
Green food colouring
142ml carton double cream
White sugar strands
24 jelly lime or lemon slices, to decorate

With a cream topping surrounded by a swirl of green lime buttercream, these zingy cupcakes are a real luxury. You can leave out one of the toppings for a lighter finish.

1 Preheat the oven to 180°C/350°F/gas 4. Stand 12 silicone cases or paper cake cases in a 12-hole muffin tin. Beat together the butter and caster sugar until pale and fluffy. Beat in the eggs, one at a time, adding a spoonful of the flour each time. Gently mix in the remaining flour, lime zest and juice.

2 Divide the mixture between the cases, filling them about two-thirds full. Bake for 15–20 minutes until golden and springy to the touch. Leave to cool completely on a wire rack.

3 For the topping, beat together the butter, icing sugar, lime juice and enough food colouring to make a soft green icing. Spoon into a piping bag fitted with a star-shaped nozzle.

4 Whip the cream until soft peaks form. Stir in the lime zest. Place a blob of cream in the centre of each cake then pipe a swirl of green icing around the edge. Sprinkle with sugar strands and decorate with jelly lime slices. Chill until ready to serve.

Dainty plum & cherry cupcakes

Prep time: 40 mins + cooling
Cook time: 20 mins
Makes 12 cakes

For the cakes:
125g (4oz) butter, softened
125g (4oz) caster sugar
2 eggs
150g (5oz) self-raising flour
3 tbsp milk
1 tbsp Amaretto
½ teaspoon ground cinnamon, plus extra,
    to dust

For the topping:
16 cherries in syrup
4 red plums
2 tbsp flaked almonds
250ml (9fl oz) double cream
½ tbsp icing sugar

Why choose between sweet cherry and almond or lightly spiced plum cakes when you can bake both in one batch? The only tricky decision is which one to try first.

1 Preheat the oven to 180°C/350°F/gas 4. Stand 12 silicone cases or paper cake cases in a 12-hole muffin tin. Beat together the butter and caster sugar until pale and fluffy. Beat in the eggs, one at a time. Stir in the flour and milk. Divide the mixture into 2 bowls. Stir the Amaretto into 1 bowl and the cinnamon into the other.

2 Drain the cherries and reserve 1 tablespoon of the syrup. Reserve 6 cherries and slice the rest. Stir the sliced cherries into the Amaretto mixture. Stone the plums. Peel and chop 2 and stir into the plain cake mixture. Slice the remainder.

3 Divide each mixture between 6 cases, filling them about two-thirds full. Sprinkle the flaked almonds onto the cherry cakes. Bake for 15–20 minutes until golden and springy to the touch. Leave to cool completely on a wire rack.

4 Whip the cream to soft peaks and divide between 2 bowls. Whisk the icing sugar into one and spoon on top of the plum cupcakes. Decorate with the sliced plums and dust with cinnamon.

5 Whisk the reserved cherry syrup into the other bowl of whipped cream and spoon into a piping bag fitted with a star-shaped nozzle. Pipe onto the cherry cakes and decorate with cherries.

Coffee cakes with mascarpone

Prep time: 35 mins + chilling
Cook time: 20 mins
Makes 12 cakes

For the cakes:
125g (4oz) butter, softened
125g (4oz) caster sugar
2 eggs
150g (5oz) self-raising flour
4 tbsp cold strong coffee

For the topping:
75g (3oz) mascarpone
200ml (7fl oz) double cream
2 tbsp icing sugar
Cocoa powder, to dust

These Italian-inspired cakes combine the wonderful flavours of a tiramisu – coffee, cocoa and mascarpone. Add a splash of coffee liqueur for an extra treat.

1 Preheat the oven to 180°C/350°F/gas 4. Stand 12 silicone cases or paper cake cases in a 12-hole muffin tin. Beat together the butter and caster sugar until pale and fluffy. Beat in the eggs, one at a time, adding a spoonful of the flour each time. Mix in the remaining flour and coffee.

2 Divide the mixture between the cases, filling them about two-thirds full. Bake for 15–20 minutes until risen and springy to the touch. Leave to cool completely on a wire rack.

3 For the topping, beat the mascarpone with 50ml (2fl oz) cream to soften then add the icing sugar and whisk vigorously until light and creamy. Whip the remaining cream to soft peaks and fold into the mascarpone mixture. Chill for 15 minutes.

4 Spoon the chilled mascarpone cream onto each cupcake and chill for about 1 hour. Dust with cocoa just before serving.

Lemon meringue cupcakes

Prep time: 30 mins + cooling
Cook time: 30 mins
Makes 12 cakes

For the cakes:
125g (4oz) butter, softened
125g (4oz) caster sugar
Zest and juice of 1 large unwaxed lemon
2 eggs
150g (5oz) self-raising flour

For the topping:
3 egg whites
Pinch of salt
200g (7oz) caster sugar
Drop of lemon juice
Strips of candied lemon peel, to decorate

This recipe uses Italian meringue which is slightly more complicated to make but is already cooked and ready to eat. You can brown the peaks under the grill if you like.

1 Preheat the oven to 180°C/350°F/gas 4. Stand 12 silicone cases or paper cakes cases in a 12-hole muffin tin. Beat together the butter, caster sugar, lemon zest and juice until pale and fluffy. Beat in the eggs, one at a time. Gently mix in the flour.

2 Divide the mixture between the cases, filling them about two-thirds full. Bake for 15–20 minutes until golden and springy to the touch. Leave to cool completely on a wire rack.

3 For the topping, whisk the egg whites and salt to soft peaks. Place the caster sugar and lemon juice in a saucepan with 50ml (2fl oz) water. Heat until the sugar dissolves, then bring to a simmer and cook until the temperature reaches 115°C on a sugar thermometer.

4 Pour the syrup onto the egg whites, a little at a time, whisking continuously. Continue whisking until the mixture is cool and standing in soft peaks.

5 Spoon the meringue into a piping bag fitted with a small plain nozzle. Pipe onto the cakes in peaks. Decorate with strips of candied lemon peel.

Chocolate & rum cupcakes

Prep time: 30 mins + cooling
Cook time: 30 mins
Makes 12 cakes

For the cakes:
125g (4oz) butter, softened
100g (3½oz) soft light brown sugar
1 tbsp rum
2 large eggs
250ml (9fl oz) crème fraîche
275g (10oz) self-raising flour
175g (6oz) milk chocolate, chopped

For the topping:
175g (6oz) milk chocolate, chopped
12 pecan nuts

These moist rum-flavoured cupcakes are studded with chocolate pieces and topped with a swirl of melted chocolate too – they're guaranteed to disappear fast.

1 Preheat the oven to 180°C/350°F/gas 4. Stand 12 silicone cases or paper cake cases in a 12-hole muffin tin. Beat together the butter, brown sugar and rum until pale and fluffy. Beat in the eggs, one at a time, followed by the crème fraîche. Stir in the flour and chopped chocolate.

2 Divide the mixture between the cases, filling them about three-quarters full. Bake for 20–25 minutes until risen and springy to the touch. Leave to cool completely on a wire rack.

3 For the topping, melt the chocolate in a heatproof bowl set over a pan of gently simmering water. Cool slightly then spread onto the cakes. Decorate each one with a pecan nut.

Fairy Cakes

Smaller and more delicate than the American cupcake, fairy cakes make a dainty teatime treat for adults and children alike. Here are some ideas to try.

Fairy cakes are made to the same basic recipes as cupcakes, but they usually have less elaborate toppings, with less icing or frosting – often just a small swirl in the centre rather than a complete, rich covering. Fairy cakes are a more delicate affair.

CLEVER CASES

Colourful silicone cases give your fairy cakes an immediate lift and look really impressive displayed on a tiered stand. Alternatively, look out for pretty patterned paper cases – available in supermarkets,

home stores and cake decorating shops. Or try the latest trend, a cake wrapper. These card strips come in lots of colours and have pretty patterns and shapes cut out of them. Simply wrap around the outside of the cakes before serving.

BRILLIANT BUTTERFLIES

Butterfly cakes are an all-time classic and it's hard to beat the basic recipe (far right); however, a few variations and additions can give this favourite cake a new look. For extra colour, brush the cut off bits of cake (or 'wings') with warmed raspberry or

Cooking with kids

Decorating cakes is always popular with children, and makes a great fun activity at a birthday party. For younger ones, stick to a simple glacé icing (icing sugar and water) that can be spooned onto the cakes. Older ones might like to try piping or swirling buttercream instead. For decorations, the sky's the limit – try a selection of colourful sweets, mini marshmallows, chopped chocolate bars, sugar sprinkles and edible glitter for starters. It just depends whether they make it onto the cakes or into little mouths first!

Fantastic icings & toppings

A simple buttercream piped or swirled on top is a classic fairy cake decoration but there are other flavours you can try too.

■ **For a dainty afternoon tea, add finely grated lemon zest to the icing and decorate with pastel-coloured sugar flowers.**

■ **For a kids' party, swirl the tops with Marshmallow Fluff (available online and from American food suppliers) or chocolate spread.**

■ **For a two-tone effect, colour half the icing in pale pink. Spoon the plain buttercream down one side of the piping bag and the pink down the other side, then pipe small swirls onto the cakes for a pretty effect.**

■ **Whipped cream makes a quick and easy topping (or filling for the Butterfly Cakes below). Flavour with your favourite liqueur, such as limoncello, Frangelico, Tia Maria, Amaretto or crème de cassis.**

Butterfly Cakes Makes 12

INGREDIENTS

For the cakes:
125g (4oz) unsalted butter, softened
125g (4oz) caster sugar
2 eggs, beaten
125g (4oz) self-raising flour, sifted
1 tsp baking powder
2 tbsp milk
1 tsp vanilla extract

For the icing:
75g (3oz) unsalted butter, softened
75g (3oz) icing sugar, sifted, plus
  extra for dusting
Coloured sugar strands, to decorate.

1 Preheat the oven to 190°C/375°F/gas 5. Stand 12 silicone cases or paper cake cases in a 12-hole muffin tin. Beat together the butter and caster sugar until pale and fluffy. Gradually add the eggs, adding a spoonful of the flour with each addition. Mix in the rest of the flour and the baking powder. Stir in the milk and vanilla extract.

2 Divide the batter between the cases and bake for 15-20 minutes until well risen and springy to the touch. Cool on a wire rack.

3 Meanwhile, beat together the butter and icing sugar until pale and fluffy. Slice off the peaked tops of the cakes with a sharp knife and slice each one in half. Add a blob of icing to the centre of each cake, then set the tops at an angle in the icing to look like wings. Decorate with sugar strands and dust with icing sugar before serving.

apricot jam then dip into hundreds and thousands to coat. Arrange on the cake. To turn a butterfly into a bunny, stand the 'wings' at one side of the cake pointing straight up to make the ears. Add a face using jelly sweets for the eyes and nose, then pipe on whiskers with icing pens or stick on pieces of liquorice or fruity laces. To make Easter chicks, cover the cakes with yellow buttercream and pipe a larger blob at one side for the head. Add the 'wings' on either side and decorate with jelly diamonds or triangles for the beaks and edible silver balls for eyes.

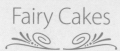

Pretty pink fairy cakes

Prep time: 30 mins + cooling
Cook time: 20 mins
Makes 12 cakes

For the cakes:
125g (4oz) unsalted butter, softened
125g (4oz) caster sugar
125g (4oz) self-raising flour, sifted
½ tsp baking powder
½ tsp salt
2 large eggs, beaten
1 tsp vanilla extract

For the icing:
250g (9oz) icing sugar
½ tsp red or pink food colouring
Assorted sugar decorations, such as
    sprinkles, sugar balls and flowers

This simple glacé icing takes minutes to make and looks really effective. Look out for different shapes and colours of sugar decorations in the supermarket baking section.

1 Preheat the oven to 180°C/350°F/gas 4. Stand 12 silicone cases or paper cake cases in a 12-hole muffin tin. Place the butter, sugar, flour, baking powder, salt, eggs and vanilla in a large bowl. Beat together with an electric whisk until smooth and creamy.

2 Spoon the mixture into the cases, filling about two-thirds full. Bake for 15-20 minutes until golden and risen. Allow to cool completely on a wire rack.

3 For the topping, whisk the icing sugar with a little hot water to create a smooth, spreadable icing. Spoon half into a separate bowl. Whisk a couple of drops of colouring into one of the bowls to make a pink icing.

4 Spread the white and pink icings on the cupcakes and decorate straight away with assorted sugar decorations. Allow the icing to set before serving.

Cream-filled butterfly cakes

Prep time: 40 mins + cooling
Cook time: 20 mins
Makes 12 cakes

For the cakes:
75g (3oz) butter, softened
100g (3½oz) caster sugar
1 large egg
100g (3½oz) self-raising flour
75g (3oz) cocoa powder
5 tbsp milk

For the topping:
142ml carton reduced-fat double cream
25g (1oz) icing sugar, plus extra, to dust
1 tbsp orange liqueur
24 raspberries

Soft cocoa-rich sponge cakes topped with indulgent liqueur cream and fresh raspberries – irresistible! You can replace the liqueur with orange zest if you prefer.

1 Preheat the oven to 180°C/350°F/gas 4. Stand 12 silicone cases or paper cake cases in a 12-hole muffin tin. Beat together the butter and caster sugar with an electric whisk until pale and fluffy. Beat in the egg, a little at a time, then mix in the flour, cocoa and milk until well combined.

2 Divide the mixture between the cases, filling them about two-thirds full. Bake for 15–20 minutes until risen and springy to the touch. Leave to cool completely on a wire rack.

3 For the topping, whip the cream with the icing sugar and liqueur until soft peaks form. Slice a small round from the centre of each cake. Spoon the cream mixture on top of the cake then cut the cake rounds in half and place on top as 'wings'. Decorate with raspberries and dust with icing sugar before serving.

Lemon fairy cakes

Prep time: 35 mins + cooling
Cook time: 20 mins
Makes 12 cakes

For the cakes:
150g (5oz) self-raising flour, sifted
125g (4oz) unsalted butter, softened
125g (4oz) caster sugar
Zest of 1 lemon
2 eggs, beaten
½ tsp baking powder

For the icing:
250g (9oz) icing sugar
Zest and juice of 1 lemon
Black poppy seeds, to decorate

With lemon in the sponge, icing and sprinkled on top, these cupcakes have a really zingy flavour. You can use orange or lime in place of lemon if you prefer.

1   Preheat the oven to 180°C/350°F/gas 4. Stand 12 silicone cases or paper cake cases in a 12-hole muffin tin. Place the flour, butter, caster sugar, lemon zest, eggs and baking powder in a bowl. Beat together with an electric whisk until smooth and creamy.

2   Divide the mixture between the cupcake cases. Bake for 15-20 minutes until golden, risen and springy to the touch. Leave to cool completely on a wire rack.

3   For the topping, whisk together the icing sugar and lemon juice with enough boiling water to make a smooth, spreadable icing. Spoon a quarter of the icing into a piping bag fitted with a thin straight nozzle. Spread the rest on top of the cakes; leave to set.

4   Sprinkle the cakes with the grated lemon zest and poppy seeds to decorate. Finally, pipe the remaining icing on top of the cakes in a swirly pattern.

Iced coconut cakes

Prep time: 30 mins + cooling
Cook time: 25 mins
Makes 12 cakes

For the cakes:
125g (4oz) butter, softened
100g (3½oz) soft light brown sugar
2 eggs
1 tsp vanilla extract
125g (4oz) self-raising flour
75g (3oz) shredded or desiccated coconut
3 tbsp milk

For the topping:
100g (3½oz) icing sugar
Red or pink food colouring
Edible pink balls and small sugar flowers,
  to decorate

These cakes have a moist, slightly chewy texture from the coconut. Decorate with flowers and balls or sprinkle with lightly toasted coconut shavings if you prefer.

1 Preheat the oven to 180°C/350°F/gas 4. Stand 12 silicone cases or paper cake cases in a 12-hole muffin tin. Beat together the butter and brown sugar until pale and fluffy. Beat in the eggs, one at a time. Stir in the vanilla followed by the flour, coconut and milk.

2 Divide the mixture between the cases, filling them about two-thirds full. Bake for 20–25 minutes until golden and springy to the touch. Leave to cool completely on a wire rack.

3 For the topping, mix the icing sugar with about 1 tablespoon of cold water to make a smooth, spreadable icing. Divide between 2 bowls and colour 1 half pink with a couple of drops of food colouring. Spoon onto the cakes and decorate with silver balls and sugar flowers. Allow the icings to set before serving.

Cinnamon-spiced cakes

Prep time: 25 mins + cooling
Cook time: 20 mins
Makes 12 cakes

For the cakes:
125g (4oz) self-raising flour, sifted
125g (4oz) caster sugar
125g (4oz) margarine, softened
2 large eggs
½ tsp ground cinnamon

For the topping:
200g (7oz) icing sugar
Red sugar flowers, to decorate

A delicate hint of cinnamon adds a beautiful aroma to these simple cupcakes. They are also good topped with buttercream or American frosting (see pages 8/9).

1 Preheat the oven to 180°C/350°F/gas 4. Stand 12 silicone cases or paper cake cases in a 12-hole muffin tin. Place the flour, caster sugar, margarine, eggs and cinnamon in a large bowl. Beat together with an electric whisk until smooth and creamy.

2 Divide the mixture evenly between the cases, filling about two-thirds full. Bake for 15-20 minutes until golden and risen. Leave to cool completely on a wire rack.

3 For the topping, whisk together the icing sugar with enough boiling water to make a thick, smooth icing. Spread over the cakes and decorate with sugar flowers. Leave to set.

Chocolate butterfly cakes

Prep time: 30 mins + cooling
Cook time: 20 mins
Makes 12 cakes

For the cakes:
100g (3½oz) butter, softened
125g (4oz) caster sugar
2 eggs
150g (5oz) self-raising flour
2 tbsp cocoa powder
4 tbsp milk

For the topping:
200ml (7fl oz) double cream
150g (5oz) raspberry jam
125g (4oz) fresh raspberries

Jam, cream and chocolate cake make a pretty irresistible combination as these dainty butterfly cakes demonstrate. They are sure to 'fly' off the plates!

1 Preheat the oven to 180°C/350°F/gas 4. Stand 12 silicone cases or paper cake cases in a 12-hole muffin tin. Beat together the butter and caster sugar until pale and fluffy. Beat in the eggs, one at a time. Gently stir in the flour and cocoa powder. Stir in the milk.

2 Divide the mixture between the cases, filling them about two-thirds full. Bake for 20 minutes until risen and springy to the touch. Leave to cool completely on a wire rack.

3 For the topping, whip the cream to soft peaks. Carefully slice the top off each cupcake with a sharp knife then cut each top in half to make the butterfly wings.

4 Spoon a little of the jam into the cenre of each cake then top with whipped cream. Stand the 'wings' in the cream and add 2 raspberries on top of each. Keep chilled until ready to serve.

Vanilla saffron cakes

Prep time: 30 mins + cooling
Cook time: 25 mins
Makes 12 cakes

For the cakes:
Pinch of saffron strands
100ml (3½fl oz) milk
125g (4oz) butter, softened
150g (5oz) caster sugar
1 tsp vanilla extract
2 large eggs
225g (8oz) self-raising flour

For the topping:
225g (8oz) icing sugar
4 tbsp milk
½ tsp vanilla extract
6 glacé cherries, halved

The addition of saffron gives these cakes a stunning yellow colour and they work really well with the sweet vanilla icing. Decorate with sugar sprinkles, if you prefer.

1 Preheat the oven to 180°C/350°F/gas 4. Stand 12 silicone cases or paper cake cases in a 12-hole muffin tin. Add the saffron to the milk and leave to stand for 5–10 minutes.

2 Strain the milk and beat together with the butter, sugar and vanilla extract until pale and creamy. Beat in the eggs, one at a time, adding a spoonful of the flour each time. Mix in the remaining flour until combined.

3 Divide the mixture between the cases, filling them about three-quarters full. Bake for 20–25 minutes until risen and springy to the touch. Leave to cool completely on a wire rack.

4 For the topping, mix together the icing sugar, milk and vanilla to a smooth, spreadable icing. Spoon onto the cakes and top each one with half a cherry. Allow the icing to set before serving.

Redcurrant fairy cakes

Prep time: 20 mins + cooling
Cook time: 20 mins
Makes 12 cakes

For the cakes:
125g (4oz) unsalted butter, softened
125g (4oz) self-raising flour, sifted
125g (4oz) caster sugar
2 large eggs
1 tsp vanilla extract
100g (3½oz) redcurrants

Fresh redcurrants add a fruity twist to these easy sponge cakes. You can use other fruits, such as raspberries or blackberries, or decorate with your favourite sweets.

1   Preheat the oven to 180°C/350°F/gas 4. Stand 12 silicone cases or paper cake cases in a 12-hole muffin tin. Place the butter, flour, sugar, eggs and vanilla extract in a large bowl. Beat together with an electric whisk until smooth and creamy.

2   Divide the mixture between the cases. Arrange the redcurrants on top of the cakes. Bake for 15-20 minutes until golden and risen. Leave to cool completely on a wire rack.

Celebration Cupcakes

A platter or tower of fancy cupcakes makes a wonderful centrepiece to any celebration and you can customise them to match the occasion or colour scheme.

Whatever the occasion – birthdays, weddings, anniversaries or parties – a show-stopping platter of cupcakes or fairy cakes is the ideal centrepiece. Change the flavour of the sponge and icing to suit your theme and use appropriate coloured sprinkles and icing to complete the look. Display on a large platter with extra sprinkles scattered around or on a tiered stand for that extra wow factor.

Campari grapefruit cupcakes Makes 12

INGREDIENTS

For the cakes:
125g (4oz) self-raising flour, sifted
125g (4oz) caster sugar
125g (4oz) margarine, softened
2 large eggs
½ tsp vanilla extract
1 pink grapefruit, peeled and chopped

For the topping:
250g (9oz) unsalted butter, softened
200g (7oz) icing sugar
125ml (4fl oz) pink grapefruit juice
75ml (3fl oz) Campari
Coloured sugar sprinkles and candy hearts, to decorate

1 Preheat the oven to 180°C/350°F/gas 4. Stand 12 silicone cases or paper cake cases in a 12-hole muffin tin. Beat together the flour, caster sugar, margarine, eggs, vanilla and grapefruit in a large bowl until smooth.

2 Divide the mixture evenly between the cases. Bake for 15-20 minutes until golden and risen. Leave to cool completely on a wire rack.

3 For the topping, beat together the butter, icing sugar, grapefruit juice and Campari in a large bowl until smooth and well mixed. Spoon into a piping bag fitted with a star-shaped nozzle. Pipe in swirls on the cakes. Decorate with sprinkles and candy hearts before serving.

GROWN-UP TREATS

Turn your pretty cakes into an adult affair with a dash of your favourite liqueur. These pretty pink cakes (above) look innocent but the icing hides a secret boost of Campari. You can experiment with flavours to create your favourite cocktails. Try coconut cakes topped with icing flavoured with coconut liqueur for piña colada cakes. Decorate with pieces of fresh pineapple and a paper umbrella. For a summer party, flavour the cakes and icing with a spoonful of Pimm's and decorate with fresh berries and mint leaves.

For a Christmas cake platter, stir some ground cinnamon and dried cranberries into your cake batter before baking. Top with cream cheese icing flavoured with extra cinnamon and decorate with icing holly leaves or snowflake sprinkles. Make your own Christmas trees by piping tall swirls of green buttercream on the cakes and decorating with sugar stars and gold or silver balls. Or make Christmas pudding cakes by turning the baked cakes out of the cases and placing, upside down, on a stand topped with white glacé icing and holly and red berries cut out of icing.

WONDERFUL WEDDINGS

For a simple, elegant display, ice the cakes with white or ivory buttercream and top with icing flowers in the same colour as the bride's bouquet. Or cut out white or coloured hearts from fondant icing and pipe on the initials of the bride and groom. For a contemporary look, decorate white iced cakes with black and silver flowers or hearts.

Special Occasions

Mark those special days with some special cupcakes.

Easter For Easter or springtime celebrations, top your cakes with pretty pastel coloured icings and decorate with sugar flowers or sugar-coated mini eggs.
Valentine's day Show your loved one how much you care with rich chocolate cupcakes topped with dark red icing. Decorate with candy hearts or cut out hearts, stars or even lips from red fondant icing. Add some edible glitter too.
Hallowe'en Create a spooky spread with green and orange marbled cakes (colour half the cake mix green and half orange with food colouring, then swirl together in the cases) topped with black icing. Cut out ghosts or pumpkins from sugarpaste.

Birthday fairy cakes

Prep time: 40 mins + cooling
Cook time: 20 mins
Makes 12 cakes

For the cakes:
125g (4oz) unsalted butter, softened
125g (4oz) caster sugar
125g (4oz) self-raising flour
2 large eggs, beaten
½ tsp vanilla extract

For the topping:
250g (9oz) icing sugar
Silver balls and sugar shapes, to decorate
12 candles

The kids will love helping to decorate their own birthday cakes with sprinkles and sugar shapes – you could even make it part of the party celebrations.

1. Preheat the oven to 180°C/350°F/gas 4. Stand 12 silicone cases or paper cake cases in a 12-hole muffin tin. Place the butter, sugar, flour, eggs and vanilla extract in a large bowl and beat together with an electric whisk until smooth and creamy.

2. Divide the mixture between the cases, filling them about two-thirds full. Bake for 15-20 minutes until golden and risen. Leave to cool completely on a wire rack.

3. Whisk together the icing sugar with enough hot water to create a smooth spreadable icing. Spread over the cupcakes and decorate with silver balls and sugar shapes before the icing sets. Add a candle to each cake just before serving.

Raspberry valentine cakes

Prep time: 40 mins + cooling
Cook time: 20 mins
Makes 12 cakes

For the cakes:
125g (4oz) self-raising flour
25g (1oz) cocoa powder
125g (4oz) butter, softened
125g (4oz) golden caster sugar
2 large eggs

For the topping:
100g (3½oz) seedless raspberry jam
300ml (½pt) double cream
Pink and red sugar sprinkles and small
candy hearts, to decorate

These rich chocolately cupcakes keep for 2–3 days un-iced in an airtight container. Once you add the fresh cream topping they are best eaten on the same day.

1 Preheat the oven to 180°C/350°F/gas 4. Stand 12 silicone cases or paper cupcake cases in a 12-hole muffin tin. Place the flour, cocoa, butter, caster sugar and eggs in a large bowl. Beat together with an electric whisk until smooth and creamy.

2 Divide the mixture evenly between the cupcake cases. Bake for 15-20 minutes until risen and springy to the touch. Leave to cool completely on a wire rack.

3 Place the jam in a bowl and stir until smooth. Add the cream and whip until soft peaks form. Spread on top of the cupcakes and decorate with sugar sprinkles and candy hearts. Serve straight away or keep chilled in the fridge.

Party cupcakes

Prep time: 45 mins + cooling
Cook time: 20 mins
Makes 12 cakes

For the cakes:
125g (4oz) unsalted butter, softened
125g (4oz) caster sugar
2 eggs, beaten
125g (4oz) self-raising flour, sifted
2 tbsp milk
1 tsp vanilla extract
1 tbsp cocoa powder
25g (1oz) dark chocolate, chopped

For the piped icing:
75g (3oz) unsalted butter, softened
2 tbsp milk
1 tsp vanilla extract
225g (8oz) icing sugar, sifted
1 tbsp cocoa powder

For the plain icing:
250g (9oz) instant royal icing
Pink and green food colouring
Small sugar flowers, leaves and sprinkles,
   to decorate

Create an impressive effect with a variety of piped and flat iced cakes. We've used chocolate and a selection of pastel colours but you can be bolder if you prefer.

1 Preheat the oven to 190°C/375°F/gas 5. Stand 12 silicone cases or paper cupcake cases in a 12-hole muffin tin. Beat together the butter and caster sugar until pale and fluffy. Gradually beat in the eggs, adding a spoonful of the flour each time. Fold in the remaining flour, milk and vanilla extract.

2 Divide half the mixture between 6 cases. Add the cocoa powder and chopped chocolate to the remaining mixture and divide between the remaining 6 cases. Bake for 15–20 minutes until well risen and springy to the touch. Cool on a wire rack.

3 For the piped icing, beat the butter until soft. Add the milk, vanilla extract and half the icing sugar and beat well. Add the remaining sugar and beat until the mixture is pale and fluffy. Divide between 2 small bowls and stir the cocoa powder into one. Colour the remaining icing or leave plain.

4 Spoon the icings into piping bags fitted with star-shaped nozzles and pipe swirls over half the cupcakes. For the plain icing, make up the royal icing as directed on the packet. Colour in as many shades as you like with a few drops of colouring.

5 Using the back of a spoon, spread a layer of royal icing over the top of the un-iced cupcakes. Allow the icing to set a little before decorating with little balls of leftover icing, edible flowers, leaves or other sprinkles.

Easy chocolate & vanilla cakes

Prep time: 30 mins + cooling
Cook time: 20 mins
Makes 12 cakes

For the cakes:
125g (4oz) butter, softened
125g (4oz) soft light brown sugar
2 eggs
150g (5oz) self-raising flour
3 tbsp milk
1 tsp vanilla extract
50g (2oz) dark chocolate, melted

For the topping:
100g (3½oz) butter, softened
200g (7oz) icing sugar

You can whip up a batch of these simply delicious cakes in under an hour! In summer, serve them topped with a scoop of ice-cream or sorbet instead of buttercream.

1 Preheat the oven to 180°C/350°F/gas 4. Stand 12 silicone cases or paper cupcake cases in a 12-hole muffin tin. Beat together the butter and brown sugar until pale and fluffy. Beat in the eggs, one at a time. Mix in the flour and milk. Divide between 2 bowls. Beat the vanilla into 1 bowl and the chocolate into the other.

2 Divide each mixture between 6 cases, filling them about two-thirds full. Bake for 15–20 minutes until risen and springy to the touch. Leave to cool completely on a wire rack.

3 For the topping, beat together the butter and icing sugar until pale and creamy. Pipe or swirl onto the cupcakes and serve.

Spring flower cupcakes

Prep time: 45 mins + cooling
Cook time: 20 mins
Makes 12 cakes

For the cakes:
125g (4oz) self-raising flour, sifted
125g (4oz) caster sugar
125g (4oz) margarine, softened
2 large eggs
½ tsp vanilla extract

For the topping:
175g (6oz) icing sugar, plus extra for
  dusting
250g (9oz) unsalted butter, softened
Green, pink, yellow and blue food
  colouring
100g (3½oz) white fondant icing
5 green, 5 pink and 10 yellow mini
  marshmallows
12 coloured sugar balls, to decorate

Gorgeous pastel shades and pretty flowers make these cakes ideal for a spring party or special birthday tea. You can vary the colours to include your favourites.

1   Preheat the oven to 180°C/350°F/gas 4. Stand 12 silicone cases or paper cupcake cases in a 12-hole muffin tin. Place the flour, caster sugar, margarine, eggs and vanilla extract in a large bowl. Beat together with an electric whisk until smooth and creamy.

2   Divide the batter evenly between the cases. Bake for 15-20 minutes until golden and risen. Leave to cool on a wire rack.

3   Beat together the icing sugar and butter until smooth and creamy. Divide equally between 4 bowls. Colour the 4 bowls of icing with green, pink, yellow and blue colouring to create pale pastel shades. Spread each icing evenly on top of 3 cupcakes.

4   Knead the fondant icing briefly to soften, then roll out thinly on a surface lightly dusted with icing sugar. Cut out 12 flower shapes with a small shaped cutters. Place one on each cake.

5   Dust a work surface with icing sugar. Place the green marsh-mallows in a line and flatten well with a rolling pin. Repeat with the pink and yellow marshmallows.

6   Place a blob of buttercream on each white flower and add the marshmallow 'petals'. Finish with a sugar ball in the centre.

Coconut & lemon cupcakes

Prep time: 40 mins + cooling
Cook time: 20 mins
Makes 12 cakes

For the cakes:
125g (4oz) self-raising flour, sifted
125g (4oz) caster sugar
125g (4oz) margarine
2 large eggs
25g (1oz) desiccated coconut
Zest of 1 lemon

For the topping:
200ml (7fl oz) double cream
100ml (3½fl oz) coconut cream
75g (3oz) icing sugar
Zest of 2 lemons, cut into fine strips

Enjoy a taste of the tropics with these delicate cupcakes topped with rich, creamy coconut frosting. Add a splash of coconut liqueur to the cream for a touch of luxury.

1 Preheat the oven to 180°C/350°F/gas 4. Stand 12 silicone cases or paper cupcake cases in a 12-hole muffin tin. Place the flour, sugar, margarine, eggs, coconut and lemon zest in a large bowl. Beat together with an electric whisk until smooth and creamy.

2 Divide the mixture evenly between the cases. Bake for 15-20 minutes until golden and risen. Leave to cool on a wire rack.

3 For the topping, place the double cream, coconut cream and icing sugar in a large bowl. Whip until soft peaks form then spoon into a piping bag fitted with a star-shaped nozzle.

4 Pipe the cream on top of the cupcakes in swirls then decorate with the strips of lemon zest before serving.

Orange-iced fairy cakes

Prep time: 30 mins + cooling
Cook time: 20 mins
Makes 18 cakes

For the cakes:
125g (4oz) butter, softened
125g (4oz) caster sugar
125g (4oz) self-raising flour
3 eggs, beaten

For the topping:
75g (3oz) butter, softened
150g (5oz) icing sugar, sifted
Zest and juice of 1 orange
Sugar flowers, to decorate

These dainty iced fairy cakes are perfect for a coffee morning, tea party or cake sale. The zingy orange icing gives them a real lift.

1 Preheat the oven to 180°C/350°F/gas 4. Stand 18 silicone cases or paper cake cases in 2 x 12-hole muffin tins. Place the butter, caster sugar, flour and eggs in a large bowl. Beat together with an electric whisk until smooth and creamy.

2 Divide the mixture evenly between the cases, filling them about three-quarters full. Bake for 12-15 minutes until well risen and golden. Transfer to a wire rack and leave to cool completely.

3 For the topping, beat together the butter and icing sugar until smooth. Add the orange zest and juice and beat to combine. Spread over the cakes and decorate with sugar flowers.

Lychee & rose cupcakes

Prep time: 35 mins + cooling
Cook time: 20 mins
Makes 12 cakes

For the cakes:
125g (4oz) butter, softened
125g (4oz) caster sugar
2 eggs
150g (5oz) self-raising flour
3 tbsp milk
1–2 tsp rose water
6 canned lychees in syrup

For the topping;
75g (3oz) butter, softened
200g (7oz) icing sugar
1–2 tsp rose water
Red or pink food colouring
12 untreated rose petals

Sweet tangy lychees give these pretty cakes an added burst of flavour. If you don't have rose petals, decorate with sugar flowers or crystallised petals instead.

1 Preheat the oven to 180°C/350°F/gas 4. Stand 12 silicone cases or paper cupcake cases in a 12-hole muffin tin. Beat together the butter and caster sugar until pale and fluffy. Beat in the eggs, one at a time, adding a spoonful of the flour each time. Gently mix in the remaining flour, milk and rose water.

2 Divide the mixture between the cases filling them about two-thirds full. Drain the lychees, chop them coarsely and divide between the cupcakes, pressing them gently into the mixture. Bake for 18–20 minutes until golden and springy to the touch. Leave to cool completely on a wire rack.

3 For the topping, beat together the butter, icing sugar, rose water and enough colouring to give a pale pink icing. Spoon into a piping bag fitted with a star-shaped nozzle. Pipe swirls on top of the cakes and decorate with rose petals.

Mini millionaire cakes

Prep time: 35 mins + cooling
Cook time: 35 mins
Makes 20 cakes

For the cakes:
125g (4oz) butter, softened
125g (4oz) caster sugar
75g (3oz) dark chocolate, melted
2 eggs
150g (5oz) self-raising flour
2 tbsp cocoa powder
4 tbsp fresh orange juice

For the topping:
125g (4oz) caster sugar
100ml (3½fl oz) double cream
40g (1½oz) butter, diced
100g (3½oz) dark chocolate, chopped

These intense dark chocolate cakes are topped with golden caramel sauce and melted chocolate. The smaller size means they are just enough without being too rich.

1 Preheat the oven to 180°C/350°F/gas 4. Stand 20 silicone cases or paper cupcake cases in 2 x 12-hole mini muffin tins. Beat together the butter and caster sugar until pale and fluffy. Beat in the melted chocolate, then add the eggs, one at a time. Mix in the flour and cocoa then stir in the orange juice.

2 Divide the mixture between the cases, filling them about two-thirds full. Bake for 15–20 minutes until risen and springy to the touch. Leave to cool completely on a wire rack.

3 For the topping, place the caster sugar in a heavy-based pan with 50ml (2fl oz) water and heat until dissolved. Bring to a simmer and cook until it turns an amber caramel colour.

4 Remove from the heat and stir in the cream. Cook for a further 2–3 minutes. Cool slightly, then stir in the butter until melted and smooth. Allow to cool.

5 Place a teaspoon of the caramel cream on each cupcake. Melt the dark chocolate in a heatproof bowl set over a pan of gently simmering water. Cool slightly then add a spoonful in the centre of each cake. Leave to set before serving.

Christmas cupcakes

Prep time: 40 mins + cooling
Cook time: 20 mins
Makes 24 cakes

For the cakes:
225g (8oz) self-raising flour, sifted
225g (8oz) caster sugar
225g (8oz) unsalted butter, softened
4 large eggs
1 tsp vanilla extract

For the topping:
500g (18oz) icing sugar
Selection of food colourings
Selection of festive sugar decorations
   (bought or home-made)

These pretty cakes work well at Christmas, as well as other times of year – try Easter ones topped with mini chocolate eggs, or Hallowe'en ones with icing pumpkins.

1 Preheat the oven to 180°C/350°F/gas 4. Stand 24 silicone cases, metallic or paper cupcakes cases in 2 x 12-hole muffin tins. Place the flour, sugar, butter, eggs and vanilla extract in a large bowl. Beat together with an electric whisk until smooth and creamy.

2 Divide the batter evenly between the cases. Bake for 18-20 minutes until golden, risen and springy to the touch. Leave to cool completely on a wire rack.

3 For the topping, place the icing sugar in a bowl and add enough boiling water to make a smooth, fairly thick, spreadable icing. Divide between 4 or 5 bowls and beat in a few drops of food colouring to colour each icing a different colour.

4 Level off any cakes that are uneven on top using a sharp knife. Spread the coloured icings evenly on top then decorate with the festive decorations. Leave to set before serving.

Using silicone bakeware

Silicone bakeware has been around for a few years now but is steadily growing in popularity, thanks to its versatility, flexibility and ease of cleaning and storing.

Silicone bakeware is a real boon in the kitchen – it's robust enough to handle the heat of the oven, the low temperatures of the freezer, bursts of energy in the microwave and the pounding of the dishwasher. Plus, it's non-stick, lightweight, flexible and easy to store.

SUCCESSFUL BAKING
Wash your silicone bakeware in warm soapy water before first using it and follow any manufacturer's guidelines for maximum and minimum temperature usage. As the pans are so flexible, it's best to stand them on a rigid baking sheet in the oven or freezer to stop any spills.

TAKE CARE!
Remember, although it cools quickly, silicone does get hot in the oven, so always use oven gloves. And don't use sharp knives or metal skewers with the bakeware as they could puncture the material.

Silicone labels
These labels explain how to use your silicone bakeware:

 Safe for use with food.

 Suitable for use in the microwave.

 Suitable for use in the freezer.

 Can be washed in a dishwasher (top shelf).

 Do not expose to direct flame.

 Do not use on the hob.

 No sharp implements.

+464°F / +240°C
-40°F / -40°C *Maximum & minimum temperatures for use.*

● When using silicone bakeware, be aware that mixtures containing certain fruits or strong colours may cause some discolouration to the moulds when baked. To reduce the risk of scorching your bakeware, make sure your oven is not too hot. When using a fan-assisted oven, reduce the temperature and cooking times according to the manufacturer's recommendation. As a guide, reduce temperatures by 10-20°C and timings by approximately 10 minutes for every hour of cooking time. Staining and scorching will not affect the performance of your silicone bakeware.

Weights, measures & temperatures

TEMPERATURE

°C	°F	Gas	°C	°F	Gas
110	225	¼	190	375	5
120/130	250	½	200	400	6
140	275	1	220	425	7
150	300	2	230	450	8
160/170	325	3	240	475	9
180	350	4			

LIQUIDS

Metric	Imperial	Metric	Imperial
5ml	1 tsp	200ml	7fl oz
15ml	1 tbsp	250ml	9fl oz
25ml	1fl oz	300ml	½ pint
50ml	2fl oz	500ml	18fl oz
100ml	3½fl oz	600ml	1 pint
125ml	4fl oz	900ml	1½ pints
150ml	5fl oz/¼ pint	1 litre	1¾ pints
175ml	6fl oz		

Please note that all conversions are approximate and have been rounded up or down for ease of use. Never mix metric and imperial measurements in one recipe.

MEASURES

Metric	Imperial	Metric	Imperial
5mm	¼in	10cm	4in
1cm	½in	15cm	6in
2cm	¾in	18cm	7in
2.5cm	1in	20.5cm	8in
3cm	1¼in	23cm	9in
4cm	1½in	25.5cm	10in
5cm	2in	28cm	11in
7.5cm	3in	30.5cm	12in

WEIGHTS

Metric	Imperial	Metric	Imperial
15g	½oz	275g	10oz
25g	1oz	300g	11oz
40g	1½oz	350g	12oz
50g	2oz	375g	13oz
75g	3oz	400g	14oz
100g	3½oz	425g	15oz
125g	4oz	450g	1lb
150g	5oz	550g	1¼lb
175g	6oz	700g	1½lb
200g	7oz	900g	2lb
225g	8oz	1.1kg	2½lb
250g	9oz		

Good practice for food safety & hygiene

- Always wash your hands before handling any food.

- Always wash fruit and vegetables before using them.

- Keep work surfaces and chopping boards clean. Keep separate boards for preparing raw meat and fish.

- Do not buy cracked eggs.

- Children, pregnant women and the elderly should not eat recipes that contain raw eggs.

- Ensure that your fridge is 5°C/41°F or less and your freezer is at least -20°C/-4°F.

- Change and wash tea towels, towels, dishcloths, aprons and oven gloves often.

- Keep pets off work surfaces and tables.

- Organise your fridge to keep raw and cooked food separately. Meat should be at the bottom, dairy produce together higher up and salad or fresh vegetables in the salad compartment.

- Store fresh food in the fridge or freezer as soon as possible after purchase.